PAPER FLIERS

Written by Alan Folder
Illustrated by Maureen Galvani
Photography by Stillview

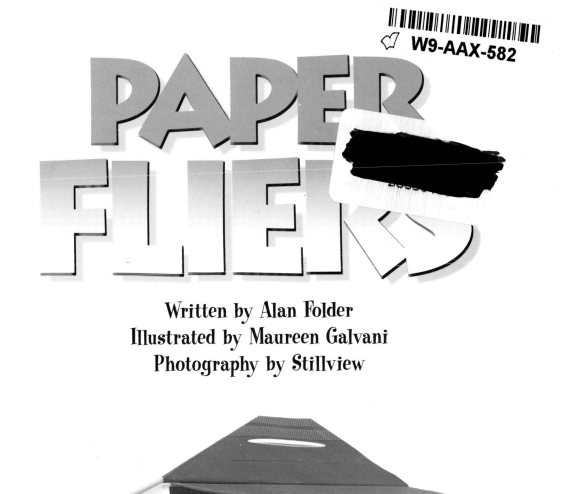

Sandy Creek

Contents

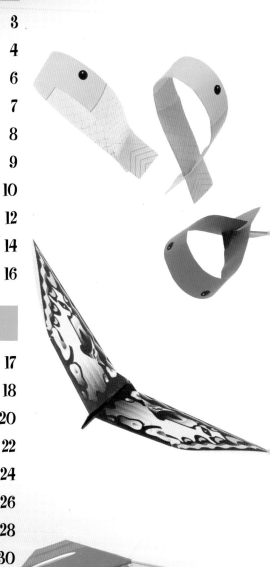

Basic Section

Advanced Section

Printed Papers

Basic
Models

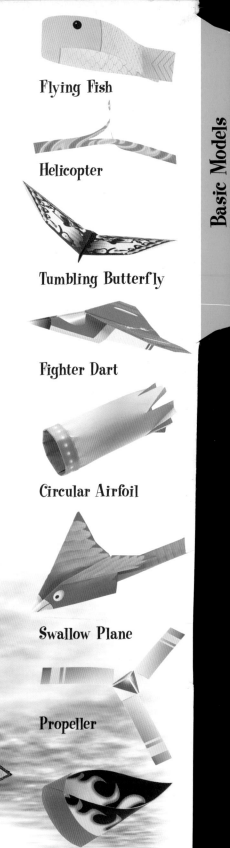

Flying Fish

Helicopter

Tumbling Butterfly

Fighter Dart

Circular Airfoil

Swallow Plane

Propeller

Gliding Ring

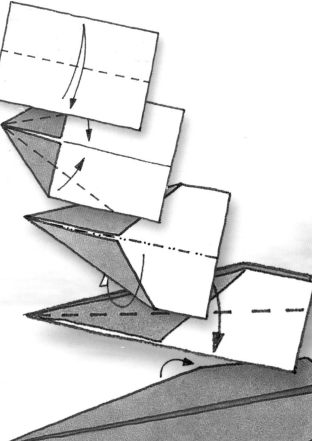

Introduction

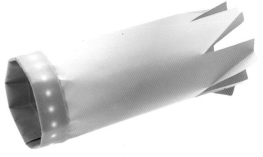

Inside this book, you will discover lots of amazing projects for you to make and fly. Also included are flying tips on how to keep your fabulous air force in the air.

The book contains pre-printed model sheets to create all of the models featured, which you will find at the back of this book in the "Printed Papers" section. Each of the printed model sheets has a number reference, which corresponds to that particular project in the "Basic" and "Advanced" sections of the book. All you have to do is remove each sheet, cut the paper to the relevant size if necessary, and you're ready to start folding! You will need a pencil, scissors, ruler, glue, the paper provided and a few other everyday things you can find around the house. It is a good idea to keep all these materials in a safe place — out of reach of any younger family members. Scissors can be very sharp, so cut carefully to avoid harming yourself or damaging any surfaces.

Remember, always be very careful NOT to hit anyone when you are throwing your airplanes.

There's lots to keep you busy as you soar into the wild blue yonder with **PAPER FLIERS!**

Folding Tips

Before you start any of the projects in this book, here are some helpful tips that will make your folding easier:

● Before you start, make sure your paper is the correct shape.

● Fold on a flat surface, like a table or a book.

● Make your folds and cuts neat and accurate.

● Crease your folds into place by running your thumbnail along them.

● Follow the instructions carefully.

Symbols & Basic Folding Procedures

The symbols in this book show the direction in which paper should be folded. Before trying any of the projects, study the following diagrams to see which way the dots, dashes and arrows go over, through and under the paper.

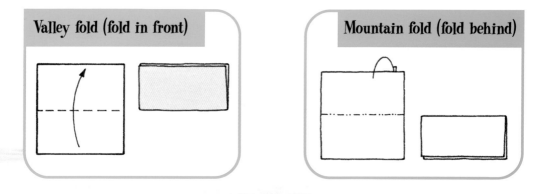

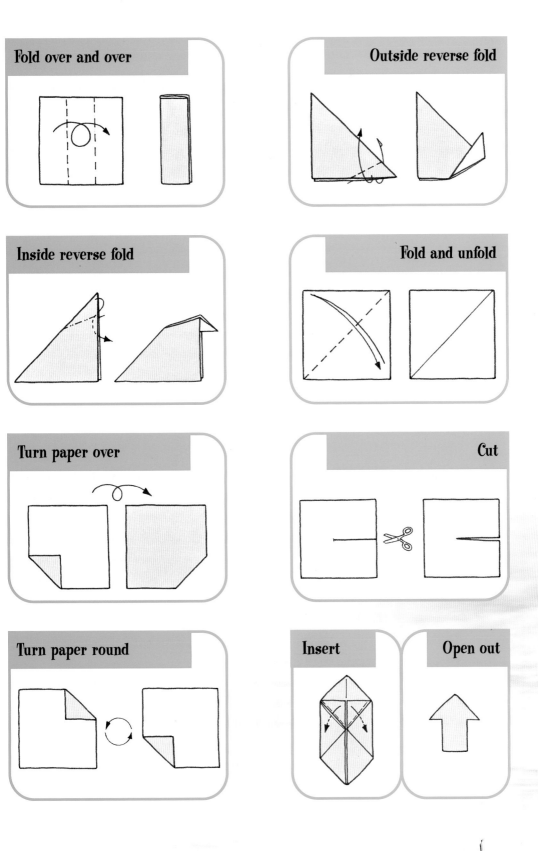

Fold over and over

Outside reverse fold

Inside reverse fold

Fold and unfold

Turn paper over

Cut

Turn paper round

Insert

Open out

Flying Fish

1 Using the paper provided (no. 1), cut long strips of paper by following the black dotted lines. Nine strips are supplied.

2 On the strip's lower right-hand side, cut a slit halfway across the strip. Repeat on the strip's upper left-hand side.

3 Bring one slit over to meet the other and...

4 ...slip one into the other, so that they are linked together. This completes the Flying Fish.

HOW TO FLY:

Throw the Flying Fish high up into the air and it will twist and turn round on its way to the ground.

Helicopter

1 Using the paper provided (no. 2), cut long strips of paper by following the black dotted lines. Six strips are supplied.

2 Make two slits in the strip, as shown, being careful each time to cut only three-quarters of the distance.

3 Bring the top and bottom ends together.

4 Fasten the two ends together with the paper clip. This completes the Helicopter.

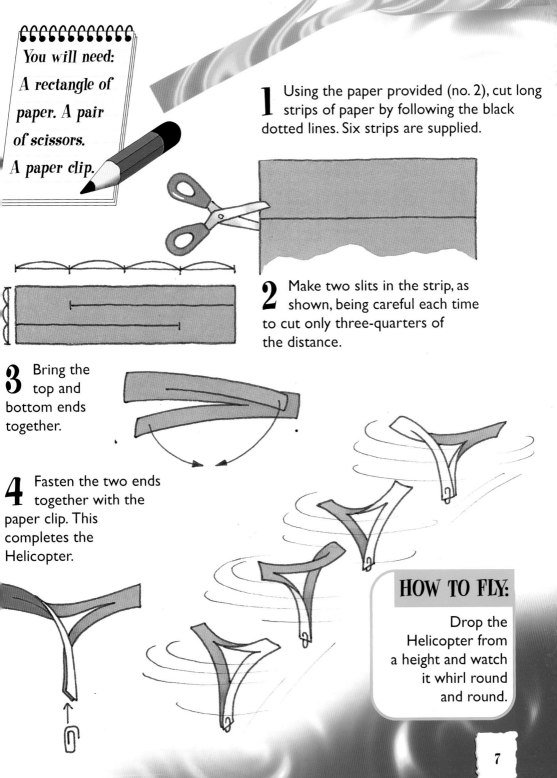

HOW TO FLY:

Drop the Helicopter from a height and watch it whirl round and round.

7

Tumbling Butterfly

You will need:
A square of paper.

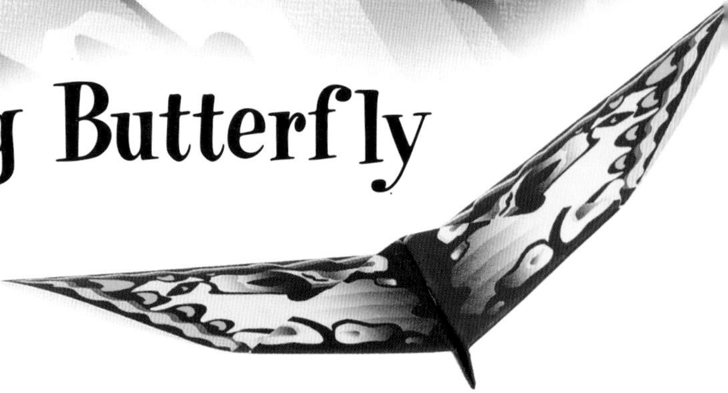

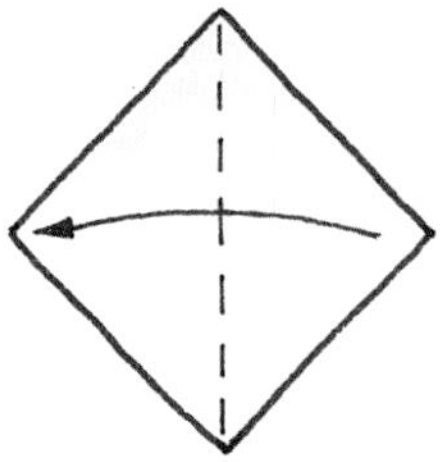

1 Using the paper provi(
(no. 3), cut away the s(
black area and discard. Pla
the square graphic-side d(
black triangle pointing rig
Fold in half from right to

2 Fold and unfold in half from bottom to top (valley fold).

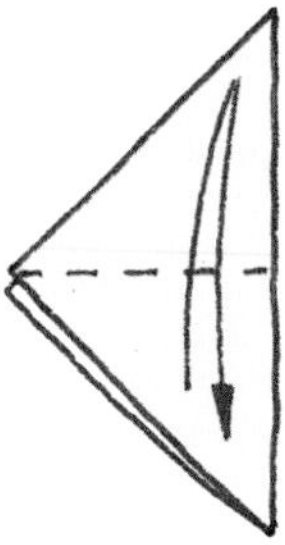

3 Fold the left-hand point over so that it overlaps the right-hand side.

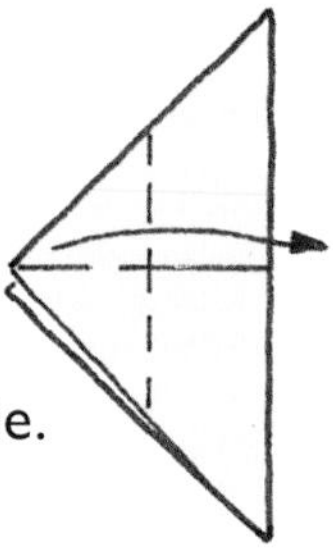

4 Fold in half from bottom to top.

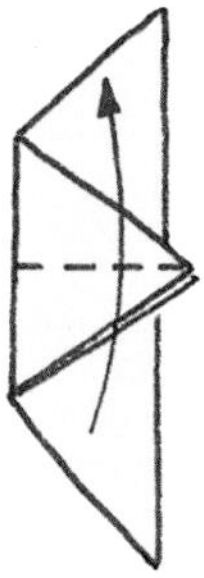

5 Fold the front flap forwards and the back flap behind, making the wings.

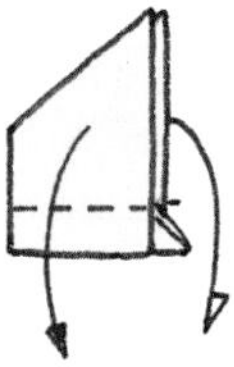

6 Lift the wings up so that they are horizontal. Open them out a little, as shown. This completes the Tumbling Butterfly.

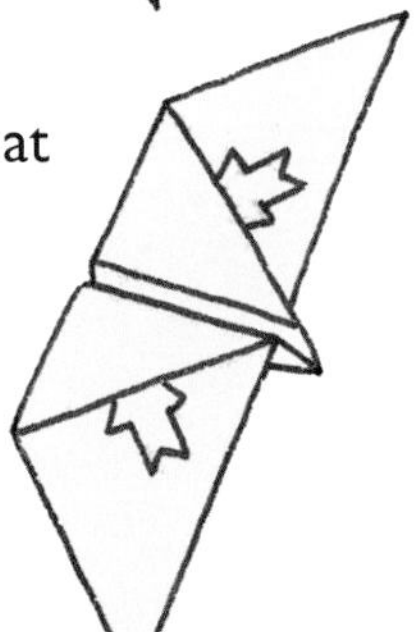

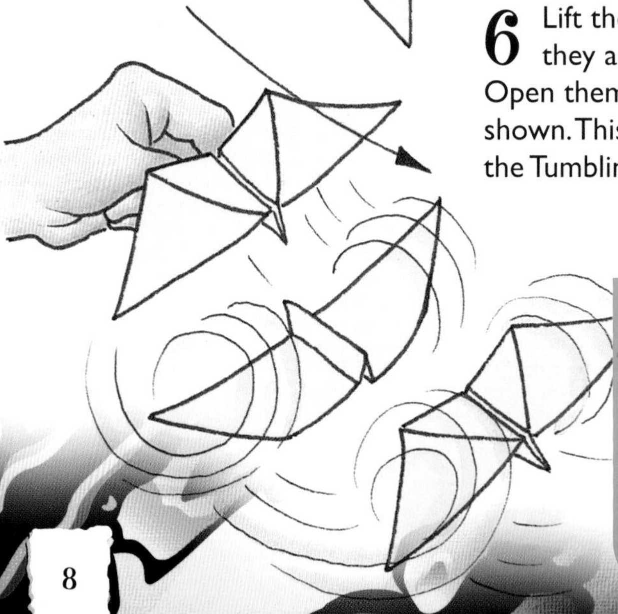

HOW TO FLY:

Hold the Tumbling Butterfly between your thumb and forefinger. Throw it forwards with a slight push up. As it falls, it will tumble over and over.

Fighter Dart

1 Using the rectangle provided (no. 4), place sideways on, white-side up, stripes on the right. Fold and unfold in half from bottom to top.

2 Fold the left-hand corners over to meet the middle fold-line.

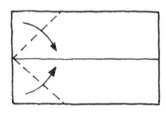

3 Fold the left-hand sloping edges over to meet the middle fold-line.

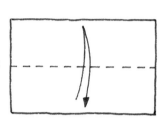

4 Fold in half, taking the paper behind from bottom to top (mountain fold).

5 Fold the front flap down and...

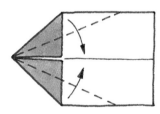

6 ...the back flap down, making the wings.

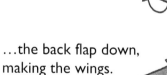

7 Lift the wings up so that they are horizontal. This completes the Fighter Dart.

HOW TO FLY:

Hold the Dart between your thumb and forefinger. Throw it firmly at a slight upwards angle.

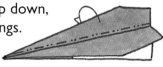

Circular
Airfoil

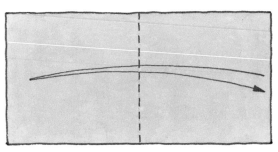

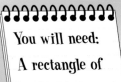

1 Using the paper provided (no. 5), place it sideways on, rainbow-effect side up, purple color to the left. Fold and unfold in half from side to side.

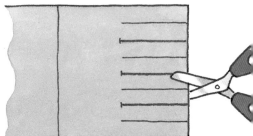

2 From the right-hand side, cut three slits in the paper, as shown.

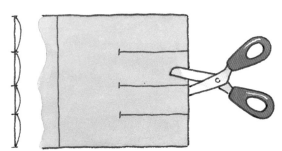

3 Again from the right-hand side, make four more slits, one on either side of those made in step 2.

4 Fold each of the slits over. Note where the fold-lines start and end.

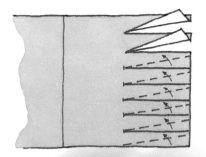

5 Fold the left-hand side over to meet the middle fold-line.

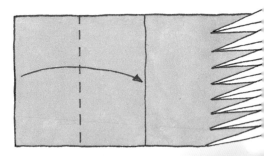

6 Again, fold the left-hand side over to meet the middle fold-line.

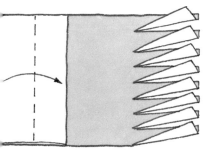

7 Fold the left-hand side over one more time to meet the middle fold-line.

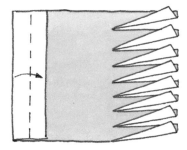

8 Turn the paper over. Bend the paper into a tube, so that the top and bottom edges slightly overlap.

9 Hold the overlapping edges in place with tape or glue. Stand the fins up straight. This completes the Circular Airfoil.

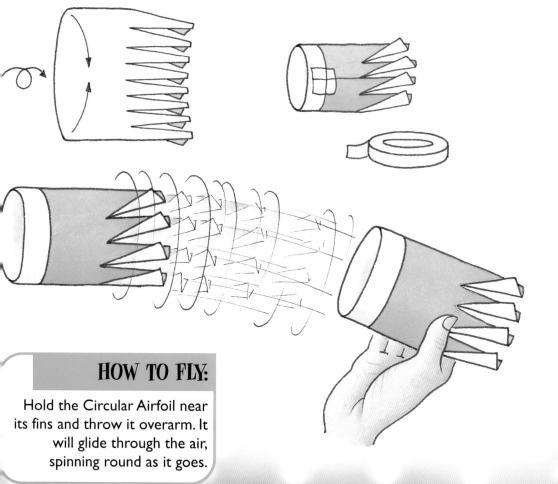

HOW TO FLY:

Hold the Circular Airfoil near its fins and throw it overarm. It will glide through the air, spinning round as it goes.

Swallow Plane

1 Using the paper provided (no. 6), cut along the yellow lines to remove the tail. Place the body square face down, feathers and eyes pointing down. Fold and unfold in half from side to side. Repeat with the tail.

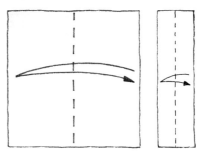

2 Fold the body's top corners down to meet the middle fold-line. Repeat with the tail strip, feathers down and nearest you.

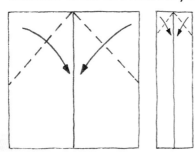

3 Fold the body's top point down, as shown.

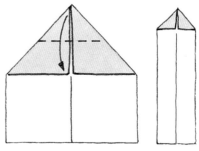

4 Fold the body down along the middle fold-line.

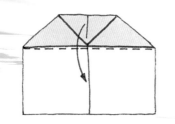

5 Tuck the tail underneath the body, as shown.

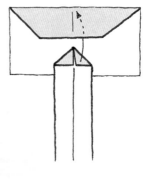

12

6 Fold the body's top corners down to meet the center fold-line, making the wings.

7 Fold the paper behind in half, from side to side, so the design is showing.

8 Turn the paper round, as shown. Fold the front wing forwards and the back wing behind. Cut off the tail's right-hand point, as shown by the shading.

9 Lift the wings up so that they are horizontal. This completes the Swallow Plane.

HOW TO FLY:

Hold the Swallow Plane between your thumb and forefinger and throw it like the Fighter Dart.

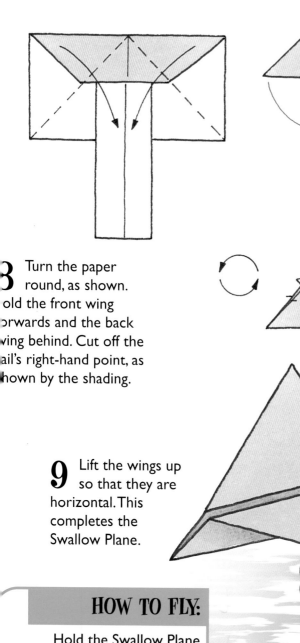

Flying Propeller

1 Using the paper provided (no. 7), cut three short strips, by following the black dotted lines. Eight pieces are provided.

2 Place the strips patterned-side down, red triangle to the left of center. Using a pencil, label the strips A, B and C. Fold each strip in half from right to left.

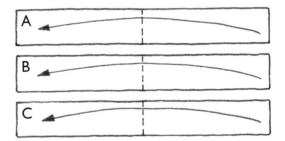

3 Take strips A and B, with the red triangles facing down, and put A inside B, as shown.

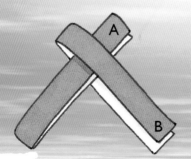

4 Weave strip C, also with the red triangle facing down, into place.

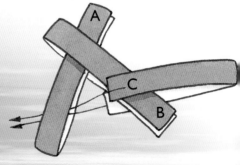

5 Pull the strips out and up in the directions shown.

A

C

B

6 Turn the strips over so the red triangles are facing upwards, and pull into a tight knot.

A

C

B

7 Fold and unfold each of the strips along the broken lines, as shown...

8 ...making them stand out from the knot. This completes the Flying Propeller.

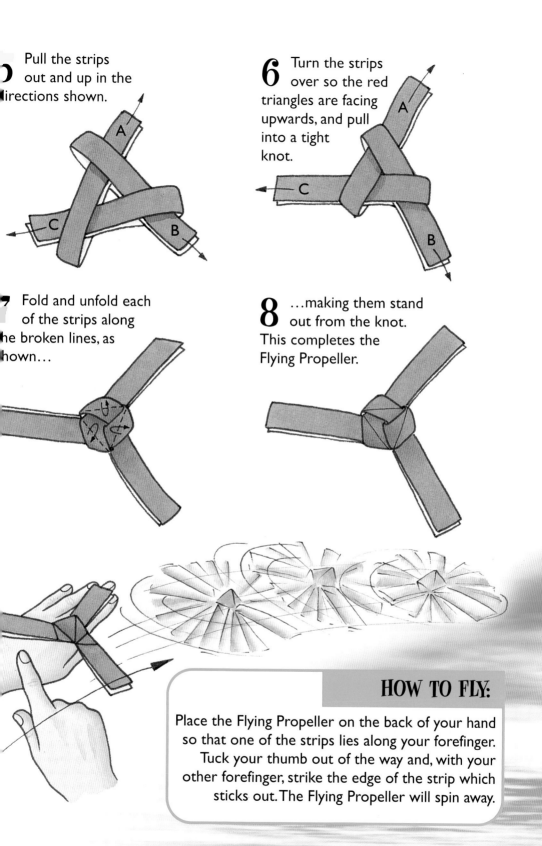

HOW TO FLY:

Place the Flying Propeller on the back of your hand so that one of the strips lies along your forefinger. Tuck your thumb out of the way and, with your other forefinger, strike the edge of the strip which sticks out. The Flying Propeller will spin away.

Gliding Ring

You will need:

A square of
paper.
Tape.

1 Using the paper provided (no. 8), cut away the solid yellow area and discard. Place graphic-side down, black at top and bottom. Fold in half from bottom to top.

2 Fold the bottom edge up...

3 ...making a small strip of paper. Turn the paper over.

4 Bring the ends of the strip up and over to meet and...

5 ...slide one into the other, making a ring-like shape. Tape in place. Curve the ring to make it as circular as possible. This completes the Gliding Ring.

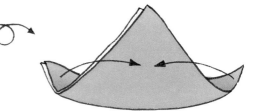

HOW TO FLY:

Hold the Gliding Ring, as shown. Throw, with a gentle push forwards, and it will travel through the air, losing height slowly.

Advanced Models

Glider

Condor

Hawk

Super Spinner

Vulcan

Hustler

Specter

Introduction to Advanced Section

Now you have mastered the basic projects, it is time to try out some of the more complicated models featured in the following pages.

When you have used up all the printed paper provided in this book, why not use plain or brown paper, and, once formed, decorate the models yourself. Try using stickers for the planes and marker pens to jazz up the models, or even glitter, stars and sequins. If you're on a tight budget, why not build up a collection of old posters or leftover wallpaper cuttings. Gift wrap from stationery stores is a good alternative or even old newspapers and magazine pages. Whatever you use, you can make your models look fantastic without having to spend all of your pocket money.

When you have made your models, why not have a competition with your friends to see whose flies the best.

Glider

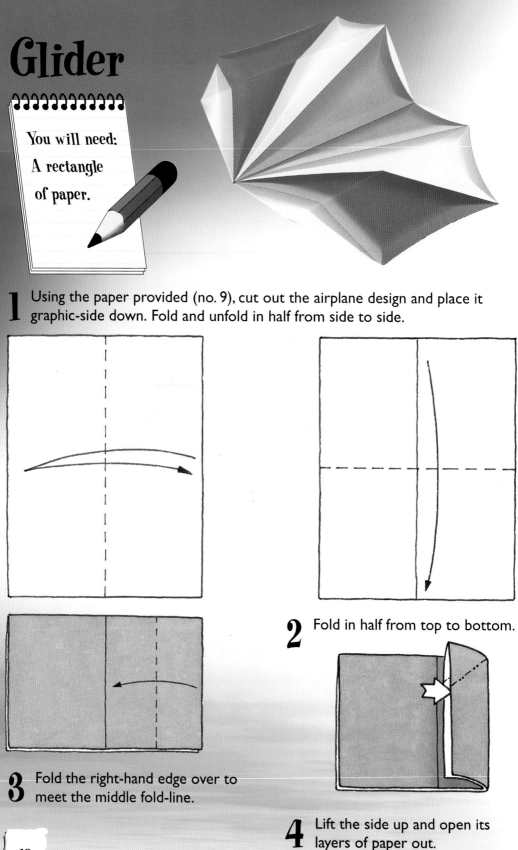

1 Using the paper provided (no. 9), cut out the airplane design and place it graphic-side down. Fold and unfold in half from side to side.

2 Fold in half from top to bottom.

3 Fold the right-hand edge over to meet the middle fold-line.

4 Lift the side up and open its layers of paper out.

5 Press the top down into the shape of a triangle. Repeat steps 3 to 5 with the left-hand side.

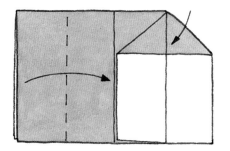

6 Fold the center panel up behind but on top of the bottom paper, to meet the triangles' bottom edges.

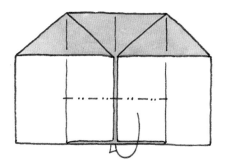

7 Fold the center panel again, tucking it underneath the triangles.

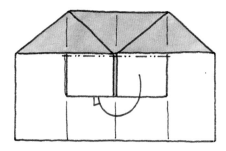

8 Next, fold the left-hand side behind to meet the right-hand side.

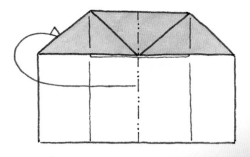

9 Turn the paper round, as shown. Fold the front flap forwards and the back flap behind, making the wings.

10 Lift the wings up so that they are horizontal. This completes the Glider.

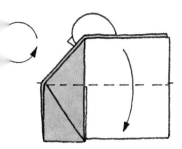

HOW TO FLY:

Hold the Glider between your thumb and forefinger and throw it gently forwards.

Condor

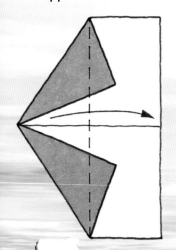

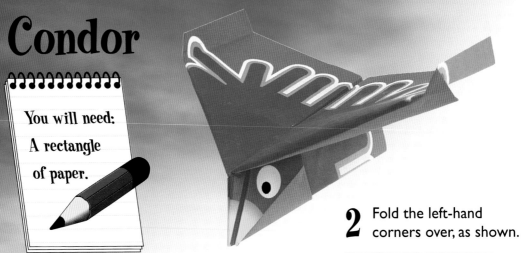

1 Using the paper provided (no. 10), place lengthways on, face down, beak to left. Fold the opposite edges together in turn, press flat and open up.

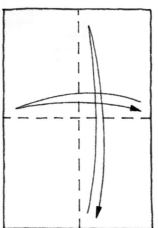

2 Fold the left-hand corners over, as shown.

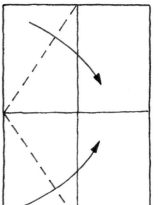

3 Fold the left-hand point over to meet the middle of the opposite side, as shown.

4 Again, fold the left-hand corners over, as shown.

5 Fold the sloping edges under, as shown.

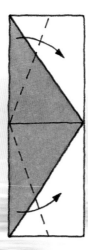

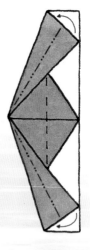

6 Fold the right-hand triangle over to the left, as shown. Fold the bottom flap behind and up to meet the top.

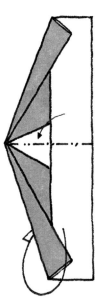

7 Fold the front flap forwards and the back flap behind, making the wings.

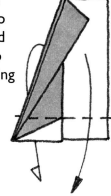

8 Fold the front wing up. Repeat behind.

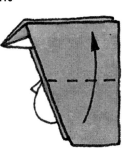

9 Fold a little of the front wing behind. Repeat with the back wing.

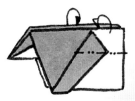

10 Open out the wings, as shown. This completes the Condor.

HOW TO FLY:

Throw high up, fairly gently, and watch the Condor float gracefully downwards.

Hawk

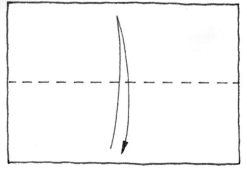

You will need:
A rectangle
of paper.
Tape.

1 Using the paper provided (no. 11), place sideways on, graphic-side down, feathers to right. Fold and unfold in half from bottom to top.

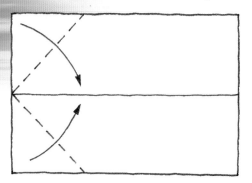

2 Fold the left-hand corners over to meet the middle fold-line.

3 Fold the left-hand point over so that it overlaps the right-hand side, with the eyes and beak visible.

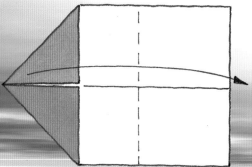

4 Fold the left-hand corners behind to meet the middle fold-line.

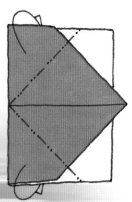

5 Fold the left-hand point over to the right, so the beak and eyes are visible.

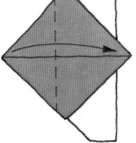

6 Fold the bottom edge behind and up to the top edge.

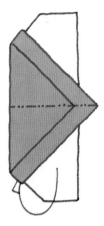

7 Fold the front flap forwards and the back flap behind, making the wings.

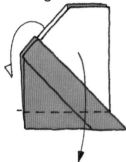

8 Fold over a little of the front wing's bottom edge. Repeat on the other wing.

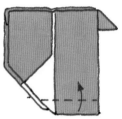

9 Open out the wings, as shown. Hold the wings together with a piece of sticky tape. This completes the Hawk.

HOW TO FLY:

Hold the Hawk between your thumb and forefinger and throw it gently forwards.

Super Spinner

1 Using the paper provided (no. 12), place it sideways on, red graphic-side down, triangles to right. Fold and unfold in half from bottom to top.

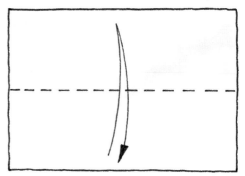

2 Fold the left-hand corners over to meet the middle fold-line.

3 Fold the left-hand sloping edges over to meet the middle fold-line.

4 Fold the left-hand point over, as shown.

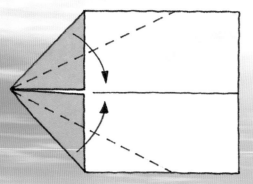

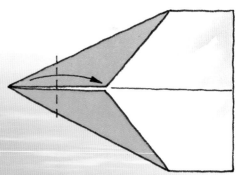

5 Fold the bottom edge behind to the top edge.

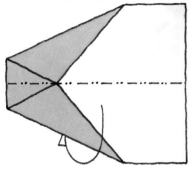

6 Push the lower right-hand corner up inside the model, as shown, making the tail.

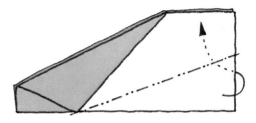

7 Fold the front flap down and the back flap down on the other side, making the wings.

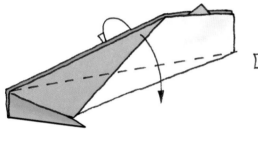

8 Lift the wings up so that they are horizontal. Hold the wings together with a piece of tape. This completes the Super Spinner.

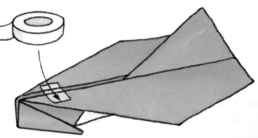

HOW TO FLY:

Hold the Super Spinner between your thumb and forefinger and throw it high into the air.

Vulcan

You will need:

A rectangle

of paper.

Tape.

1 Using the paper provided (no place it sideways on, flames d facing right. Fold and unfold in ha from bottom to top.

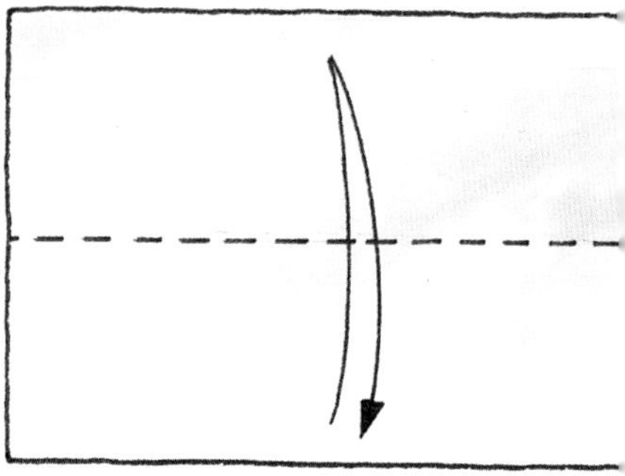

2 Fold the left-hand corners over to meet the middle fold-line.

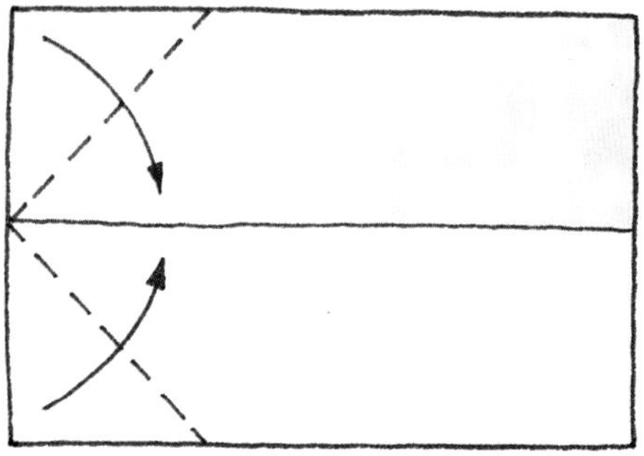

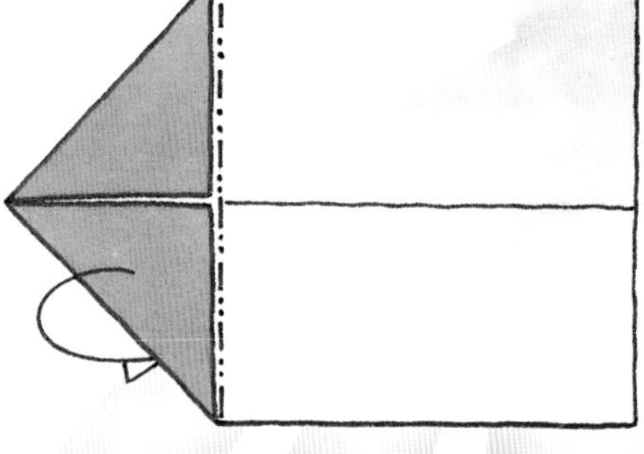

4 Fold the left-hand side over one-fifth of the way to the right, to where the red print are meets the black.

3 Fold the left-hand point behind, as shown.

26

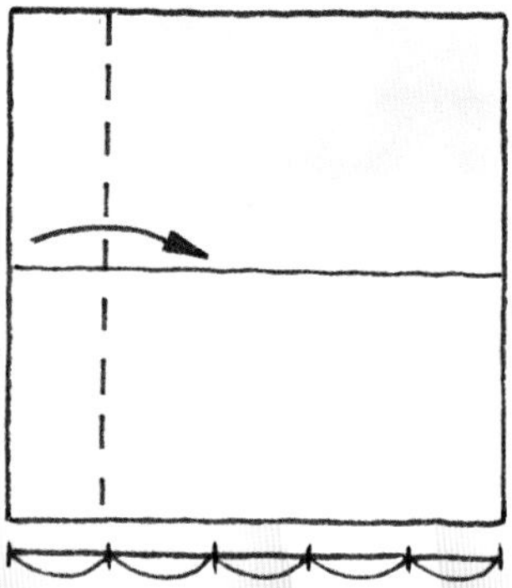

5 Again, fold the left-hand corners over to meet the middle fold-line.

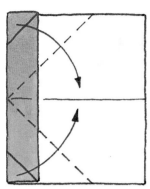

6 Fold in half from bottom to top.

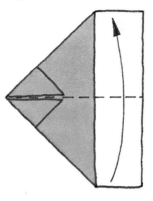

7 Fold the front flap down. Repeat on the other flap.

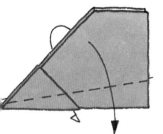

8 Fold the front flap up at an angle, and repeat with the back flap, making the wings, as shown.

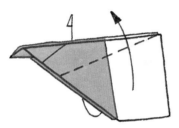

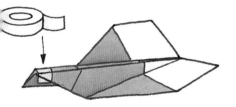

9 Open out the wings, as shown. Hold the folds together with a piece of tape. This completes the Vulcan.

HOW TO FLY:

Hold the Vulcan between your thumb and forefinger and throw it fast and straight ahead.

Hustler

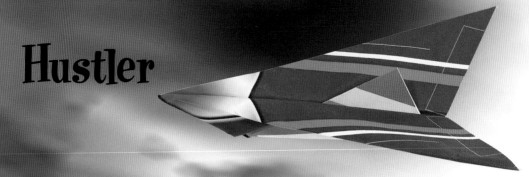

You will need:

A rectangle of paper.

Tape.

1 Using the paper provided (no. 14), place sideways on, triangle on top, pointing down. Fold and unfold in half from side to side.

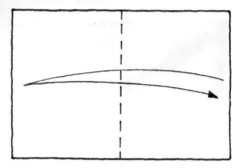

2 Fold the bottom corners over diagonally to meet the middle fold-line, as shown.

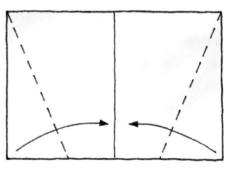

3 Fold the bottom edge up, as shown.

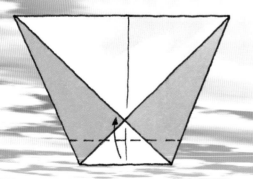

4 Fold the bottom edge over, along the adjacent edge.

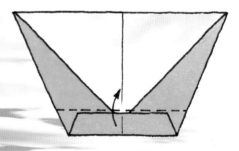

5 Fold the sides over diagonally to meet the adjacent edges, as shown.

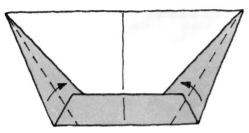

6 Fold the sides over along the adjacent edges to meet the middle fold-line.

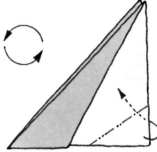

7 Fold the plane in half so the parts meet on the backside.

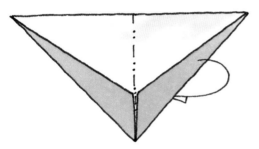

8 Turn the paper round, as shown. Push the lower right-hand corner up inside the model, making the tail.

9 Fold the front flap down, as shown, and repeat with the back flap, making the wings.

10 Open out the wings, as shown. Hold the folds together with a piece of tape. This completes the Hustler.

HOW TO FLY:

Hold the Hustler between your thumb and forefinger and throw it firmly, straight ahead.

Specter

1 Using the paper provided (no. 15), place it sideways on, graphic-side down, triangles to the right. Fold and unfold in half from bottom to top.

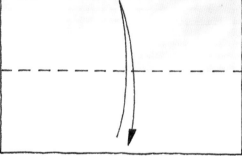

2 Fold the left-hand corners over to meet the middle fold-line.

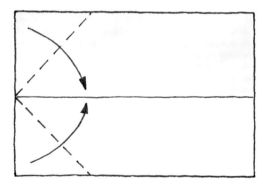

3 Fold the left-hand point over to meet the middle of the opposite edge, as shown.

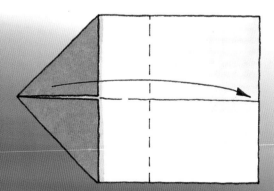

4 Again, fold the left-hand corners over to meet the middle fold-line.

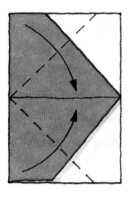

5 Fold the small right-hand triangle over towards the left.

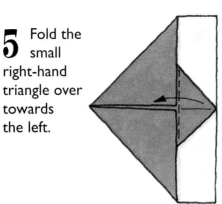

6 Fold the left-hand point over towards the right and...

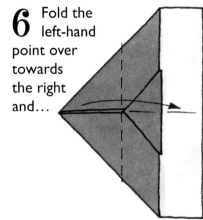

7 ...tuck it up inside the model.

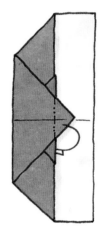

8 Fold the bottom edge behind to the top edge.

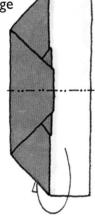

9 Push the lower right-hand corner up inside the model, as shown, making the tail.

10 Fold the front flap down and repeat with the back flap, making the wings.

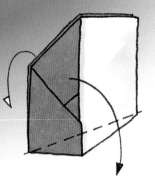

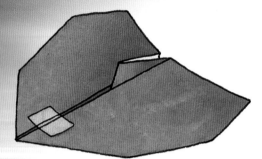

11 Open out the wings, as shown. Hold the folds together with a piece of tape. This completes the Specter.

HOW TO FLY:

Hold the Specter between your thumb and forefinger and throw it firmly, straight ahead.

Printed Papers

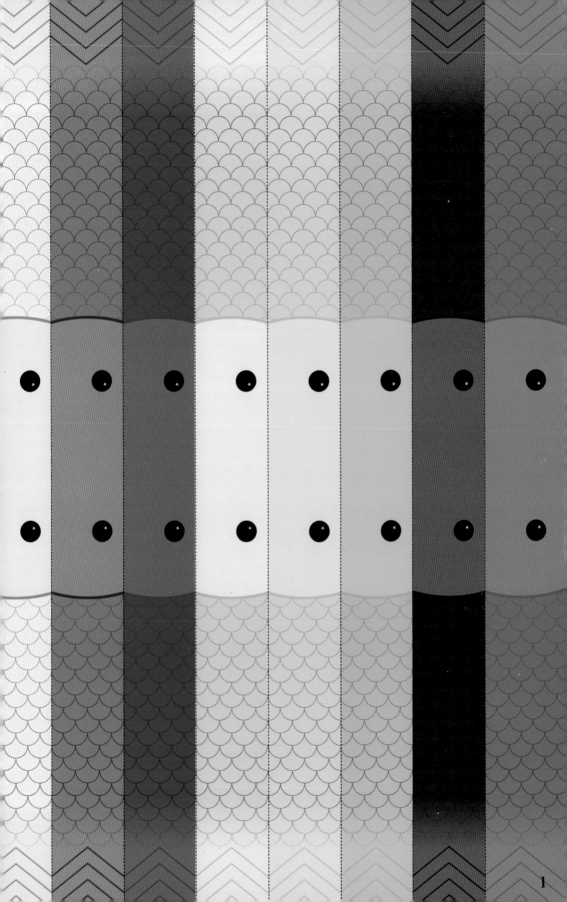

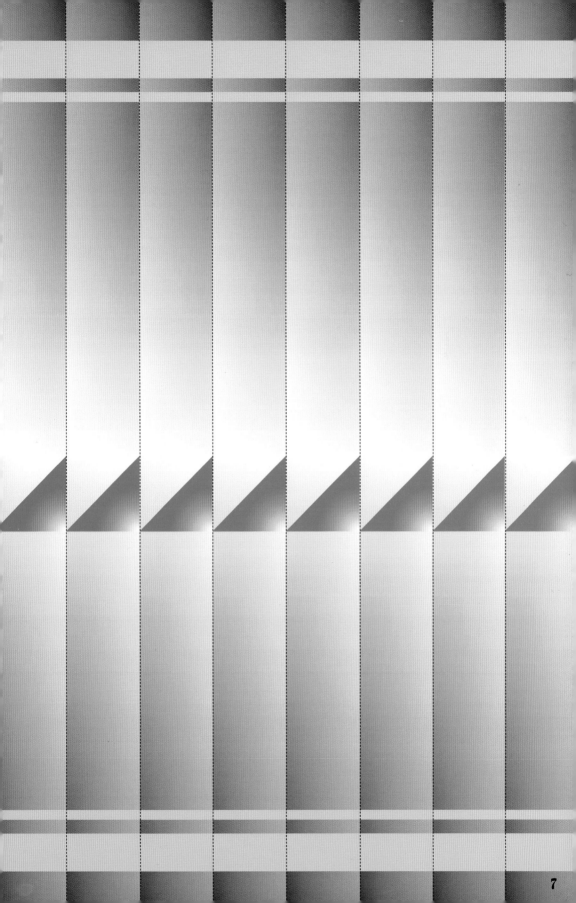

Spare

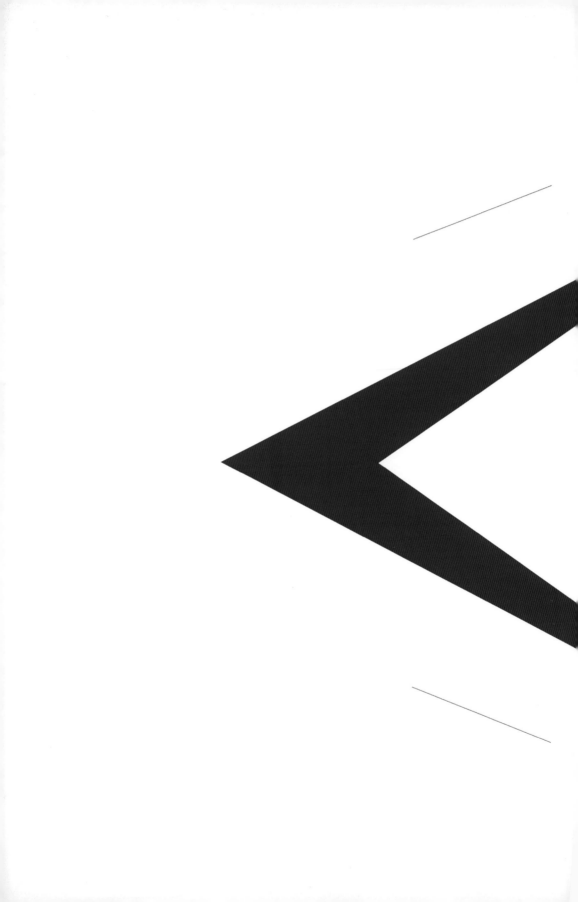